Jets
AND
BOMBERS

POSTER
BOOK

by Bill Holder
and John Farquhar

Willowisp Press

GLOSSARY

Air superiority fighter This plane rules the sky by being the best at flying fast and turning quickly.

Bomber This is a large, multi-engine plane that has a mission to deliver weapons on an enemy target.

Delta formation This six-plane grouping is triangular in shape. It is a regular formation of the Thunderbirds.

Demonstration team These are planes that fly together to put on air shows. The Thunderbirds and Blue Angels are the two most famous teams.

Dogfighter This is a fighter airplane that can go up into the air and bring down enemy airplanes. The F-16 Fighting Falcon is an example of this type of plane.

Fighter This is a single-person airplane that is built to clear the skies of enemy aircraft and also to help army troops on the ground.

Formation This is a perfectly formed group of four to six airplanes, usually fighters.

Mach number Mach 1 is the speed of sound. The Mach number indicates how fast an airplane can fly. It's the ratio of the speed of an aircraft to the speed of sound.

Maneuvers This is when an airplane moves around the sky by changing the positions of parts of its wings and tail.

Reconnaissance This is a military exploration to gather secret information about enemy territory for national defense. A plane on one of these missions flies high and takes pictures of the gound far below.

Sidewinder missile This small missile is carried by fighters to destroy enemy planes.

Cover photos by U.S. Air Force

Published by Willowisp Press, Inc.
401 E. Wilson Bridge Road, Worthington, Ohio 43085

Copyright © 1989 by Willowisp Press, Inc.

Printed in the United States of America

The F-16 is used by the U.S. Air Force Thunder-birds. Quick and powerful, these Fighting Falcons are perfect for the maneuvers performed by this famous team. Six-plane formations, like this delta, are the most difficult to do. The fancy paint jobs on the bottom of the Thunderbird F-16s show a bird design.

Flying almost straight upward at high speeds, the F-15 Eagle is the U.S. Air Force's hottest fighter. The Eagle has two powerful jet engines and is fully loaded for air-to-air combat. Its job is to fight at high altitudes, which is why it is called an air superiority fighter plane.

The giant B-52 Stratofortress bomber weighs almost a half million pounds with all the fuel and weapons that it carries. Its eight jet engines burn a lot of fuel. To keep the B-52 in the air for its long-distance missions, the bomber must refuel now and then. A KC-135 jet tanker fills up the B-52 so that it can keep flying for hours longer.

Hundreds of F-16s are now flying in the U.S. Air Force, as well as in the air forces of many other countries. Here is a formation of three Fighting Falcons. Each plane is carrying sidewinder missiles on its wing tips. These missiles can be fired at enemy airplanes that are attacking the F-16s.

The U.S. Air Force uses the F-111 because it is a big and fast fighter plane. The F-111 was one of the first planes to have a wing that can move while the plane is in flight. The faster the F-111 flies, the further back the wing is swept. Fully swept back, the plane looks like an arrowhead.

Bright red Tutor airplanes fly in tight formations with the Canadian Snowbirds air demonstration team. The Snowbirds are exciting, and they perform their shows with nine planes filling the skies in front of the crowds. The Snowbirds don't fly as fast as the American teams do, but their formations and stunts are just as thrilling.

The Blue Angels is the U.S. Navy's famous flight demonstration team. The Angels use the A-4 Skyhawk jet fighter plane. Like the Thunderbirds, the Blue Angels fly very close together in their diamond formations. The planes are beautifully painted in dark blue with yellow trim.

This large and beautiful B-1B is America's newest bomber. It has four powerful engines under the body, and wings that can move during flight. The B-1B has a crew of four, and it can carry many different kinds of weapons. The B-1B can fly fast at very low and very high altitudes.

This strange formation by two Thunderbird F-16s is part of the team's show. One Fighting Falcon is hanging upside down directly over an upright plane. This is very risky business, and everything has to be exactly right. The team trains for many hours to make every show perfect.

The Thunderbirds fly in formation only three to four feet apart when they are flying at 600 miles per hour. That's very dangerous, but this team does it carefully and skillfully. The planes also can produce smoke trails to paint their paths across the high skies.

This F-16 Fighting Falcon is looking at you almost straight on. It weighs only 16,500 pounds, which is very light compared to other fighters. This dogfighter is very quick and can turn on a dime. The F-16 Fighting Falcon is used by the air forces of many countries.

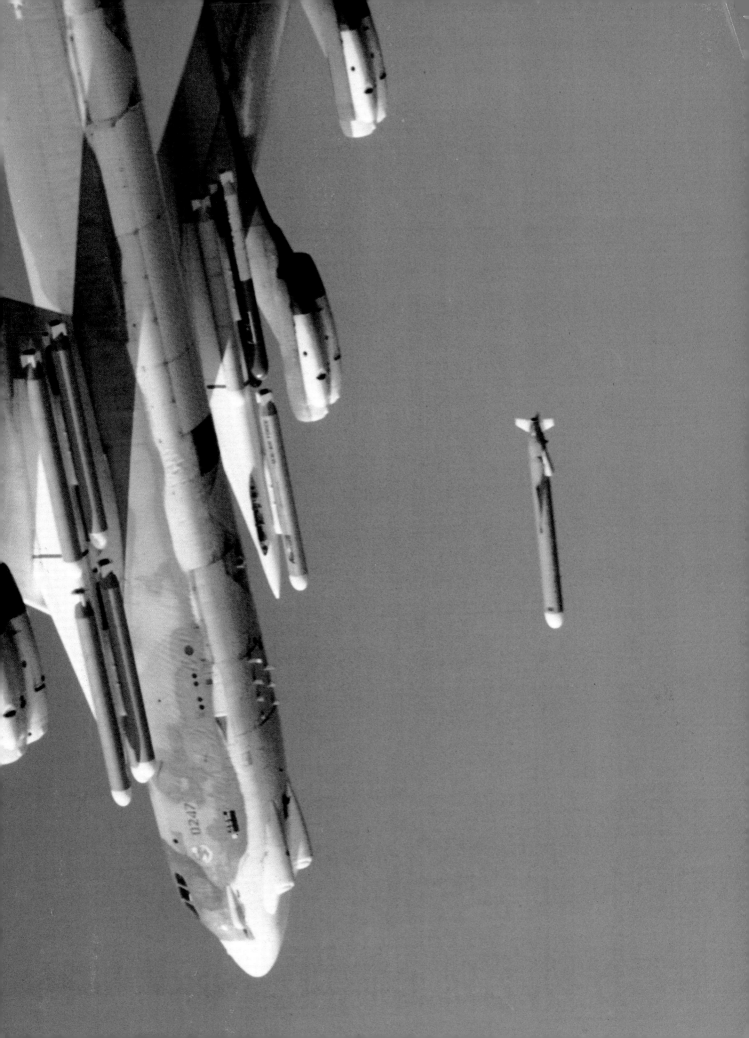

The B-52 can carry a huge load of different types of weapons. One type is the air-launched cruise missile, or ALCM. The ALCM is dropped from the B-52's wing, or out of the plane's body. The ALCM's air-breathing engine starts up and pushes the missile to a far away target.

Canada and the U.S. Navy fly the F-18 Hornet, the newest and most advanced jet fighter. The plane has two engines that can power the Hornet with 32,000 pounds of push. This picture shows a view from the rear cockpit of an F-18 of the Canadian 409th Tactical Fighter Squadron.

This wild-looking plane is able to fly at Mach 3, which is three times the speed of sound, and at about 16 miles high. The SR-71 Blackbird was built for reconnaissance, or photo-taking missions for national defense. This American super sleuth has been flying for over 20 years, and it is still one of the hottest airplanes.

Springing off the deck of an aircraft carrier, this F-14 Tomcat fighter pours on the power in a screaming climb. Aboard the two-seater plane are the pilot and the radar intercepter officer (RIO), who sits in the back and is in charge of radar and weapons. The Tomcat was the star of the movie *Top Gun.*